# THE EXECUTIVE

# THE
# EXECUTIVE
## MAKE MY LIFE LESS GREY

First published in 1961 as The Executive Coloring Book by
The Funny Products Company

This edition first published in the US in 2017 by G. P. Putnam's Sons, an imprint
of Penguin Random House LLC

This edition first published in Great Britain in 2017 by
Michael O'Mara Books Limited
9 Lion Yard
Tremadoc Road
London SW4 7NQ

A CIP catalogue record for this book is available from the British Library.

Papers used by Michael O'Mara Books Limited are natural, recyclable products
made from wood grown in sustainable forests. The manufacturing processes
conform to the environmental regulations of the country of origin.

ISBN: 978-1-78243-818-2 in hardback print format

1 2 3 4 5 6 7 8 9 10

www.mombooks.com

Cover design by Ana Bjezancevic
Typeset by Ana Bjezancevic

Printed and bound in China

This book is humbly dedicated to Marcie Hans, Dennis Altman and Martin A. Cohen

# THIS IS MY COLOURING BOOK

**My name is** _____

**My company is** _____

**My title is** _____

**My next title will be** _____

**THIS IS ME.** I am an executive. Executives are important. They go to important offices and do important things.
Colour my underwear important.

**THIS IS MY SUIT.** Colour it grey or I will lose my job.

**THIS IS MY ATTACHÉ CASE.** It helps people know I am an executive. It makes me look efficient. Organized. Competent. I wonder if it opens.

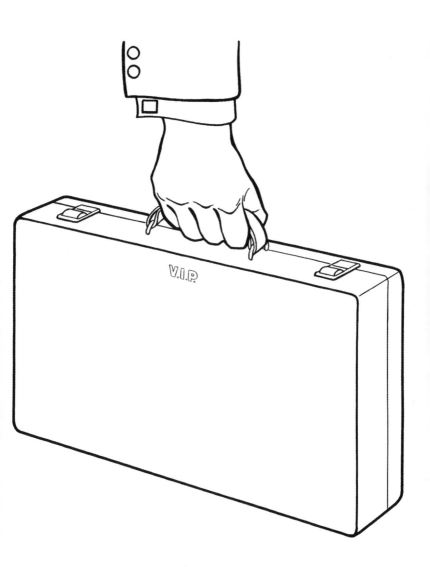

THIS IS MY TRAIN. It takes me to my office every day. You meet lots of interesting people on the train. Colour them all grey.

THIS IS MY ELEVATOR. It takes me way up high. People who are not executives stand right next to me in my elevator. They are all right, but I would not want my daughter to marry one of them.

THIS IS MY DESK. It is mahogany. Important people have mahogany desks. My walls are mahogany, too. I wish I were mahogany.

THIS IS MY TELEPHONE. It has five buttons.
Count them. One, two, three, four, five.
Five buttons. How many buttons does
your telephone have? Mine has five.

THIS IS MY COMPANY'S PRESIDENT. He hates me. He calls me bad names, but he gives me lots of raises. My wife calls him 'Papa'.

THIS IS MY SECRETARY. I hate her. She is mean. I used to have a soft, round lady. But my wife called her 'Papa'.

THIS IS MY WIFE.

**THIS IS THE PRODUCT MY COMPANY MAKES.**
It is an inter-fibrous friction-fastener.

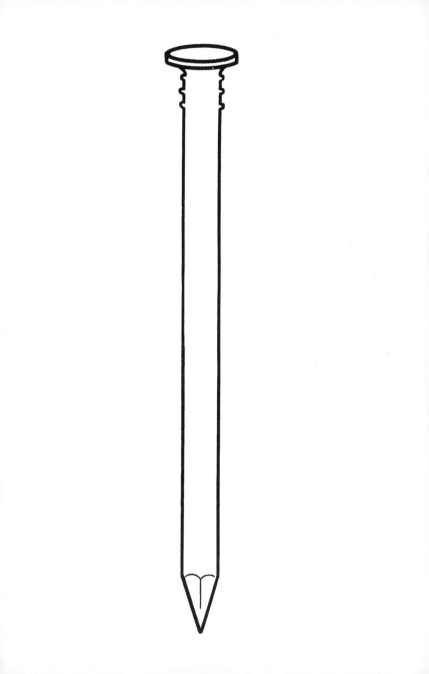

THIS IS OUR COMPETITOR'S PRODUCT. It is a nail.

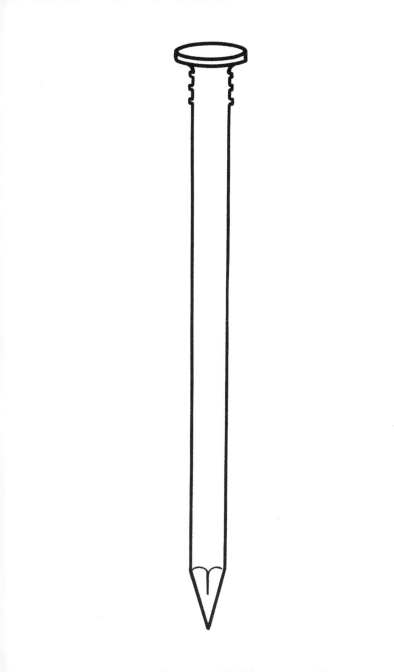

**THIS IS MY COMPANY'S LUNCH ROOM.** Sometimes I walk through it and smile at the employees. 'Hello, employees,' my smile says, 'I am one of you.' I never eat there.

THIS IS MY SALES CHART. When the line goes up, I feel good. When the line goes down, I get gas. Colour me green.

**THIS IS MY PILL.** It is round. It is pink. It makes me not care.

Watch me take my round, pink pill

… and not care.

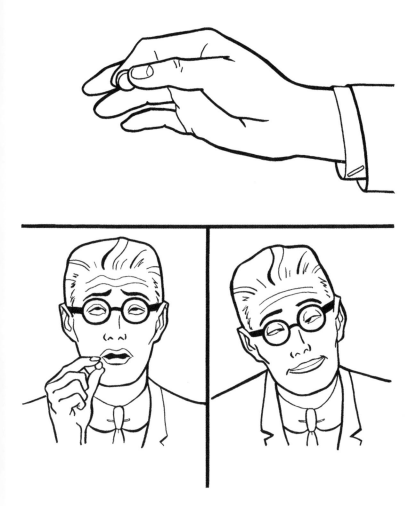

THIS IS MY SECRET.

**THIS IS A CUSTOMER.** He smells bad. He has money to spend. I like him.

**THIS IS MY CAR.** It is a company car. It is used for deliveries only.

**THIS IS MY MINK COAT.** I take it to my club. I take it to banquets. It goes lots of places with me. My wife comes, too.

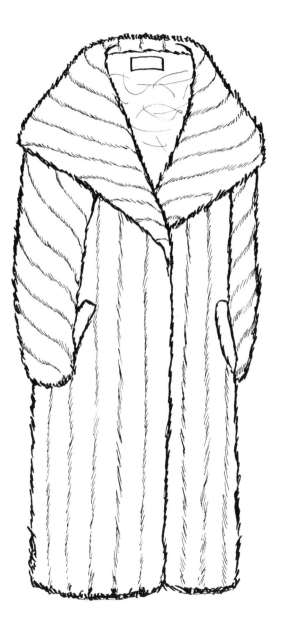

**THIS IS MY SIGNATURE.** It is big. It is hard to read. Some people have little signatures that are easy to read. They never make over a hundred a week.

Furthermore notwithstanding heretofore consequently, stock option. Business-wise general picture debenture. Sales picture tax loss henceforth. Net worth.

Amortize co-operate firm up cost-plus employee relationship profit picture. Simultaneously depletion allowance company policy heretofore solidify. Corporate bond industrial outlook. Inventory profit straightforward profit margin complaint heretofore without prejudice.

Budget non-recurring phenomenon co-operate option. General picture labor problem annuity, inventory kickback subsequently nonetheless.

Fiscal year notwithstanding company policy gross mark up. Debenture solid front. Government percent draft re-order renewable. Contractually solid front.

With best personal regards to Mildred and the children.

Very truly yours,